SOAKING
ENCOUNTER
—— JOURNAL ——

SOAKING
ENCOUNTER
— J O U R N A L —

*An Interactive Journaling
Experience with the Holy Spirit*

CAROL ARNOTT

DESTINY IMAGE® PUBLISHERS, INC.

P.O. Box 310, Shippensburg, PA 17257-0310

"Promoting Inspired Lives."

This book and all other Destiny Image and Destiny Image Fiction books are available at Christian bookstores and distributors worldwide.

Cover design by Eileen Rockwell
Interior design by Terry Clifton

For more information on foreign distributors, call 717-532-3040.

Reach us on the Internet: www.destinyimage.com.

ISBN 13 TP: 978-0-7684-5476-5

For Worldwide Distribution, Printed in the U.S.A.

1 2 3 4 5 6 7 8 / 24 23 22 21 20

CONTENTS

INTRODUCTION

Do you ever feel stuck in an endless cycle of everything you have on your plate? Is your to-do list a mile long? When is the last time you just stopped to be with Jesus? Without an agenda, without a prayer list, without all your worries and concerns? Do you know the Saviour of the whole world is deeply in love with you? He wants to fill your life with His love and His presence every single day. This soaking journal will take you on a journey with the King of kings, the King of your heart. It is an invitation to go deeper with Him and let His love transform your life.

I really believe in the power of prayer ministry. Over the years, my husband, John, and I have seen that people who take time to receive prayer after a sermon in a church service receive a lot more than just hearing the message and going on with their day. I think the same applies to reading books. You have an opportunity to let the message go from your head to your heart. That's why I have written this journal to go along with my book, *Soaking in the Spirit: Effortless Access to Hearing God's Voice, Intimacy with the Father, and Supernatural Healing*. The prompts and questions in this journal will guide you into a deeper level of soaking and encountering God. As you go through the journal, don't be in a rush. Allow the Holy Spirit to encounter you each time you soak.

We all get so busy doing. Life seems to throw a million things at us at once. It's so easy to become tired and burnt out and weary in well doing. Soaking is the antidote to that. It is an opportunity to abide in the presence of God. Soaking is purposefully making space to be together with the Lord and to receive from Him. The more time we spend in His presence, experiencing Him, the more we will be filled with Him and it will never be a waste of time. You can't give away what you haven't already received from Him. That means you need to take the time to receive!

Soaking literally changed my life. I've learned and experienced that abiding in God's presence will totally transform your relationship with your Saviour, your Bridegroom, and your King, and it will empower you to bring the kingdom with mighty signs and wonders. Because of the way my life has been deeply transformed through soaking, I want to share my experiences with you. I want you to meet Jesus through soaking and fall more in love with Him every day. I want you to be equipped by the Holy Spirit for the good works God has prepared for you to do.

In John 15, Jesus tells us to abide in Him. That's not a suggestion; that's a command. We all want to lead fruitful Christian lives, but first, we must spend time with Jesus. Abiding comes first. That's where we become anointed and filled to do what Jesus is calling us to do. We need to be filled up with God's love and presence so that we can love Him and love others. That's our whole purpose. If you're not filled up, then you can't give anything away, and if you don't give anything away, that's not healthy either. You become like stagnant water. There must be a constant flow of love in our lives.

We can't love God or others well if we're weary or burnt out. So we need to make time to love Him and to connect with Him. That is what soaking is all about, making that time to connect with Him. Soaking helps keep us in balance with loving God, others, and ourselves. Soaking is positioning yourself before God, just to be together with Him intimately. Intercession and prayer are so important and valuable, but there must always be time to experience His love for you and to give Him your love with no expectations or agendas.

When you come to soak, don't come with a shopping list of your needs. Instead, come to tell Him that you love Him, that you want to go deeper with Him. His heart's desire is to love you back and to go deep with you too. As you spend time in His presence, you'll begin to see how real He is. You'll see that He wants to have a wonderful relationship with you, that intimacy is His heart's desire. Jesus paid the highest price for you so that you might draw close to Him.

As we love on Him, we get filled up with His love and we begin to love Jesus back. Receiving His love for us helps us love Him more. Each time you soak it will be different. Sometimes He'll flood you with His unconditional love and acceptance. Sometimes He'll heal a wound in your life. Sometimes you'll feel the heavy, weighty presence of God so much that you can't move. It's all valuable and it's always worth making time for.

This journal includes some questions to ask yourself, some questions to ask God in prayer and journaling, and some practical applications and prayers. Take time to let God speak to you and transform you; again, do not be in a rush, allow the Holy Spirit to speak to you. When you get an impression as you soak, write it down on these pages. It's good to write down the things that He tells you so that you can pray them back, ponder them, and meditate on them. You will find that by the time you finish this journal, you will have written a beautiful new story with the Lord. I pray as you continue on in this journal, you will allow the Lord to meet you on every page. Let's jump right in and get started.

SECTION 1

STILLNESS AND SOAKING

MOST PEOPLE NEED TO LEARN HOW TO BE STILL IN the presence of God. They're used to filling the silence with their worship and prayer. It's so important to find a quiet, still space to make room to hear God speaking and to recognize His presence. Once you're comfortable, close your eyes and welcome the Holy Spirit. Fix your eyes on Jesus and tell Him that you love Him and want to spend time with Him.

Music helps set a peaceful atmosphere as you soak. I love to start with worship music that draws my heart to loving Jesus. As you sing to Him, it will help you focus in on Him and bring your heart into peace. Starting with adoration and worship will help you take your focus from the distractions and busyness of life and onto Jesus.

As you worship and feel the presence of the Lord permeating you, welcome Him even more. Recognize His presence with you. Tell Him that you love Him and you want to spend time with Him. Then allow Him to take the lead. Take time to just be silent and listen for His still, small voice. Ask Him what He wants to do today and what He wants to show you.

I want to be
so filled with
His love that
I radiate it
to everyone
I meet.

Psalm 139:17 (NIV) says, *"How precious to me are your thoughts, God! How vast is the sum of them!"* Today as you soak, take time to ask Him what He wants to say to you about you. He's never lost for words toward you.

We each need
to have the
fragrance of
intimacy in
our own lives.

WHEN YOU BEGIN TO SOAK, YOUR MIND WILL GO nuts. As soon as you make a quiet space, you'll all of a sudden remember all the things you need to do and all the things you've forgotten. When distractions come, take a piece of paper, write it down, and go back to soaking. If the thoughts of everything you have to do are causing you stress, picture yourself giving them to Jesus as you write them down. Take a deep breath and ask Him to take care of those things and to show you what to do with them after you've finished soaking.

> As I learned to pour out my love on Him and soak in His presence, I received a deep and lasting understanding of His love.

TRY TO PUT YOUR OWN AGENDAS ASIDE AND LET yourself be His beloved. Ask the Holy Spirit where He wants to take you today and welcome His presence. You'll be surprised where He takes you. Write down what you see and sense during this soaking session.

_____

_____

_____

_____

_____

_____

_____

> Scripture says, *"Be still, and know that I am God"* (Psalm 46:10). It doesn't say, "Accomplish a lot and know that I am God."

_____

_____

_____

_____

_____

_____

_____

_____

IF GOD SEEMS TO BE REPEATING HIMSELF, DON'T GET frustrated. Simply ask Him why. It could be that God wants to remind you of His heart for you until you really believe it.

Soaking opens up the heart and soul to romance and intimacy with the Lord.

In Matthew 7, Jesus says, *"Ask, and it will be given to you; seek, and you will find; knock, and it will be opened to you. For everyone who asks receives, and he who seeks finds, and to him who knocks it will be opened"* (Matthew 7:7-8). As you seek the presence of the Holy Spirit, He is delighted to show Himself to you. Keep asking Him for more. It's that simple prayer that we learned to pray when the revival began: "More, Holy Spirit!"

_____

_____

_____

_____

_____

_____

_____

_____

_____

_____

> The more I received God's presence, the more I soaked Him in, the more fruit I saw in my life.

_____

_____

_____

_____

For many people, it helps to stay still, but if you struggle to focus when you're still, then you can still soak while you're on the move. You can quiet yourself down and tune your mind to what the Holy Spirit is saying and doing while you go for a walk, ride your bike, or exercise at the gym. If that's you, try listening to Him while on the move. When you get home, write down what He showed you.

He wants to be together in the significant moments and the little day-to-day moments when nobody else is watching.

ACTIVATION AND PRAYER

What are your challenges to connecting with God's presence and resting with Him?

Do you tell yourself, "I'm not good at resting" or, "I'm just not built to sense and feel the Holy Spirit," or, "I'll always be distracted"? If that's you, tell Him:

Lord, here I am. I repent of believing that because of my character or personality, I can't spend time resting with You, or that I can't receive from You. Lord, I want You, whether or not I feel anything. I position myself in faith to receive from You.

SECTION 2

GETTING TO KNOW
THE HOLY SPIRIT

I WANT TO INTRODUCE YOU TO THAT WONDERFUL third Person of the Trinity, the Holy Spirit. Like me, you may be aware of God the Father, and Jesus, the loving Son and Bridegroom, but less acquainted with the Holy Spirit.

The Holy Spirit is a Person. He is gentle, forgiving, and long-suffering. He is called the Comforter and He truly is the most wonderful friend and companion. In John 16, we see that the Holy Spirit brings the words of Jesus to our remembrance and convicts the world of sin. He guides us into all truth; He is the Spirit of truth and the giver of life. He is our Teacher. He will help you understand the Bible and lead you in your prayer life. He wants to communicate with you. Just ask Him, "Holy Spirit, teach me how to pray." He always knows what to say.

The Holy Spirit helps us to love Jesus and to know the Father. He is the most wonderful Person, yet He is holy and also very powerful! His power raised Jesus from the dead and He empowers us to live an abundant, joyful, powerful Christian life. Spend time today reflecting on your thoughts about the Holy Spirit. Who is He to you?

Kathryn
Kuhlman
would say,
*"He's more real
to me than any
human being."*

THE HOLY SPIRIT IS A PERSON. HE IS GENTLE, FORGIVing, and long-suffering. He is called the Comforter and He truly is the most wonderful friend and companion. Do you know the Holy Spirit as a companion and a friend? As you soak, ask the Holy Spirit to come as your friend. Ask Him what He wants to show you today and write it down.

_____

_____

_____

_____

_____

_____

_____

_____

_____

_____

_____

_____

_____

_____

_____

_____

The Holy Spirit was there at creation, hovering over the waters. He was present throughout the Bible and He is still with us. He is around us, He can fill us, and He can come on us in power.

AS YOU GROW DEEPER AND DEEPER IN YOUR RELA-tionship with the Holy Spirit, He will ask you to do things. As you choose obedience, you'll build with Him and learn to trust Him more. Today, ask the Holy Spirit if there is anything specific He wants you to do. Even if you don't hear anything right now, be aware of His prompting as you go through your day. Maybe He will give you a word of encouragement for someone or ask you to pray for healing for someone. Get ready for a wonderful adventure as you follow His lead!

It pleases the Holy Spirit when we love Jesus and when we bear good fruit. He actually enables us to become like Jesus—full of love, joy, peace, patience, kindness, goodness, faithfulness, gentleness, and self-control. His presence in your life will cause you to be more thankful, more loving, and more unified with others.

SOMETIMES PEOPLE BELIEVE THAT TO EXPERIENCE the Holy Spirit you need to have a big physical manifestation. If they don't feel something strong, they think God is not moving. Did that ever happen to you? One way the Holy Spirit touches you is through His peace. Stay still and ask the Holy Spirit to come right now. Do you feel peace? Welcome that peace and ask for more. Jesus is the Prince of Peace and experiencing peace is a wonderful manifestation of His presence.

_____

_____

_____

_____

_____

_____

_____

"The peace of God, which transcends all understanding, will guard your hearts and your minds in Christ Jesus" **(Philippians 4:7 NIV).**

_____

_____

_____

_____

_____

_____

If we want to please the heart of God, it's so important to recognize that the Holy Spirit has feelings. When we are critical and judgmental of others, when we're proud, when we're bitter, and when our words aren't pleasing to the Father, it grieves Him (see Eph. 4:30). Ask the Holy Spirit to reveal your thoughts and your heart because it's so easy to be critical and judgmental. Give Him permission to speak into your life and ask Him if you've hurt Him. Write down anything He reveals to you.

_____

_____

_____

_____

_____

_____

_____

_____

In these end times, the Holy Spirit wants to come in power, and He wants people He can trust who are sensitive and aware of His presence.

_____

_____

_____

_____

_____

_____

IT HURTS THE HOLY SPIRIT WHEN WE DON'T LOVE each other like He loves us. We're called to forgive everybody. Of course, forgiveness is not the same as trust. We can forgive and ask for love for a person who has hurt us, but that doesn't mean that you have to trust a person who has hurt you deeply. Today, pray and ask the Holy Spirit if there is anyone in your life you need to forgive. Release them to God and receive peace and freedom.

> I was filled with the love, joy, and peace of God's presence and I didn't want it to stop there.

R.T. Kendall talks about the Holy Spirit as a dove who is easily hurt and very sensitive. Bill Johnson talks about the Holy Spirit as a dove that rests on your shoulder. How would you behave if you had a real dove sitting on your shoulder and you didn't want it to fly away? You'd be very aware of all of your movements and very careful about what you said. Today as you soak, picture the Holy Spirit like a dove sitting on your shoulder. Keep this in mind as you go through your day.

Have you ever experienced that you feel more of the Holy Spirit as you worship? That's because He wants you to worship Jesus. The more we love Jesus, the more the Holy Spirit will come.

ACTIVATION AND PRAYER

Do you feel like you relate to God more as Father, Son, or Holy Spirit? Take some time to ponder and ask God whether you've been unaware of the wonderful third Person of the Trinity.

Invite Him to move in your life again. Do you want to be filled with the Holy Spirit? To have a deep relationship with Him? To abide with Him? Simply ask God: "Father, I want to be immersed in that wonderful presence. Help me to know the wonderful Person of the Holy Spirit." Take time to wait on Him and abide with Him today.

Where has control or fear become a barrier to you experiencing the Holy Spirit? Repent for those decisions today. Tell Him,

> *"God, I want to feel and to experience You. Teach me, nurture me in feeling and experiencing Your presence. I welcome You to move in my life."*

SECTION 3

HEARING GOD'S VOICE

ONE OF THE BIGGEST BENEFITS OF SOAKING IN GOD'S presence is getting to know His voice. I love Mark Virkler's teaching on hearing God's voice. In the early days of our church, God spoke clearly to John that there were some important values that we needed at the core of our ministry, including teaching how to hear God's voice. We got connected with Mark Virkler, who had spent a year searching the Scriptures for a clear guide to hearing God speak and found four simple keys out of Habakkuk 2:1-2. When someone learns to hear God's voice for themselves, it completely changes their relationship with Him. It becomes living and active.

Many of us hear the devil loud and clear and our own thoughts loud and clear, but don't know how to listen for the still, small voice of the Lord, unless we're taught how to. Soaking teaches us to quiet ourselves down to find the gentle voice of God. As you spend this time soaking and developing your relationship with God in a new way, you will hear His voice more and more clearly.

Jesus only did what He saw the Father doing and only said what He heard the Father speaking. In order to follow that example and live like Jesus did, we need to know God's voice. When we understand that God speaks and that often it's in a gentle voice, we're able to honor those little thoughts that come into our minds and we're more likely to do something about it. This week we will go through the keys that God showed Mark and practice hearing His voice. Today as you soak, ask God to make His voice more and more clear to you.

> Your whole
> life will change
> when you
> realize that the
> Lord absolutely
> loves you.

KEY 1: THE FIRST KEY THAT MARK VIRKLER TEACHES is to quiet yourself down. Soaking teaches us to quiet ourselves down to find the gentle voice of God. Of course, He can speak loudly, but most of the time we experience Him in a whisper, like Elijah, rather than in a loud voice. In lives that are so full of busy clatter, quieting ourselves down is really important. Practice this quietness as you soak. (Remember you can use a notebook to write down any distractions then get right back to stillness.)

_____

_____

_____

_____

_____

_____

_____

_____

_____

> If we as a church don't learn to be intimate with Him now, what is it going to be like when we get to heaven as His bride?

_____

_____

_____

_____

KEY 2: MARK VIRKLER'S SECOND KEY TO HEARING God's voice is to fix your eyes on Jesus. Soaking is all about focusing on your Beloved. It's taking your eyes off the rest of life to adore Him and commune with Him. As you soak today, focus on Jesus and ask Him to show you another facet of who He is to you.

I didn't know that I needed to be "born again," but that night I said yes to Jesus and gave my life to Him. From then on, it was a wonderful adventure getting to know Him.

KEY 3: MARK TEACHES THAT WE MUST TUNE IN TO spontaneous thoughts. As you take time to soak today, pay attention to the spontaneous thoughts in your mind. Could it be that some of your seemingly random thoughts are actually from the Lord? The more you practice, the easier it will be to distinguish His voice from your thoughts. Soaking helps you learn to hear God through your thoughts and through the eyes of your heart.

> Can you imagine what would happen if all believers could walk as Jesus walked?

KEY 4: MARK TEACHES THAT WE NEED TO WRITE down and record everything that God says, so that we can be accountable with two others as we learn to hear God and so that we have a record to look back on. Throughout this journal, you have been writing down what God is speaking to you. If you sense something, but you don't know if it is God's voice, there are a few ways to test this. First, it must line up with the Word of God. Next, you can talk to a friend or mentor in your life about what you sensed. Ask them to pray with you and let you know if it seems right to them. This is especially important for major life decisions like moving to a new place, job choices, or relationships.

When the Holy
Spirit works in
our lives, He
brings dramatic
transformation.

So many times, I've had people tell me, "I was soaking, and I thought about so-and-so, so I made a note and called them later." It turned out that the person was in a crisis or really needed encouragement. That's the voice of God putting that person in your mind. When you're soaking today, ask God if there is anyone He wants you to reach out to today. Ask Him if there is anything specific He would want you to tell that person.

> The Holy Spirit knows what everyone is going through and wants to put people on your heart to love them and pray for them.

BEFORE I STARTED SOAKING, I NEVER HAD A VISION. I also believed that I didn't dream. Then I realized that God loves to speak to people through dreams. I quickly repented and asked God to speak to me through dreams and visions. Just as Mark Virkler teaches, we must allow God to speak to us through pictures. God wants to use the eyes of your heart. Dreams and visions are a really important part of the way that God wants to speak to us. We see them throughout the Bible. Ask God to begin to give you more dreams and visions. Write them down and ask God what He wants to reveal to you through these dreams and visions. You can start practicing today; as you soak, ask God for a vision from Him. What did He bring to mind?

It's possible for all of us to hear God through dreams and visions.

ACTIVATION AND PRAYER

This week, we practiced soaking using Mark Virkler's keys to hear God's voice—quieting yourself down, fixing your eyes on Jesus, tuning in to spontaneous thoughts, and writing down what He says. These keys help guide your soaking to hear God's voice even more clearly.

As you hear God speak more and more, you build trust. You trust that He is always speaking to you, and you also trust yourself to discern what is coming from God and what is coming from your own mind. Jesus followed His Father's voice completely. To live like Jesus, in perfect union with the Father, we need to know our Father's voice.

Do you hear His voice clearly? Do you struggle with distractions, negative thoughts or self-criticism? Ask God to quiet down all other voices and make His voice the loudest. He is speaking love and life over you. If you relate to this, pray:

> *God, I hear so many other thoughts, making it hard to hear Your voice clearly. Lord, please quiet all the distractions and all the negative thoughts. Help me to hear Your voice, the voice of a loving Father who is speaking life over every situation I face. Thank you that You love to speak to Your children, and I choose to believe You are speaking to me too.*

SECTION 4

LETTING GOD HEAL YOU THROUGH SOAKING

OUR CULTURE DEMANDS THINGS TO BE INSTANT. We're used to getting everything we need straightaway. We can become that way with Jesus. We want Him to instantly fix our problems, our finances, our emotional trauma, and our physical ailments. In reality, all these things require commitment. Knowing Jesus intimately doesn't happen at the click of a finger. It's the same with healing emotional trauma. It takes time for your heart to be healed. You get a measure of healing, then you walk that out, and then the Holy Spirit will deal with more. It's so important to make time for the Lord to heal your wounds. I urge you to prioritize the healing of your heart.

Through our experiences with God in Toronto and around the world, we also learned that the same principles can be true for physical healing. Sometimes God does the miracle in an instant, but many times, it comes through persistent prayer and soaking prayer. We have seen incredible miracles as people soaked in God's presence. Sometimes that happens during the course of one evening, other times it happens over years. I personally went through three years of struggling with significant health issues. It was a difficult time for me, but I persisted in prayer and learned the value of soaking through all seasons. Whether you need a physical healing or deeper healing of your heart, are you willing to take the time to let God touch you in His way? Will you trust that as you soak, He is working in your life whether you see results instantly or only over time?

He keeps
us leaning
on Him,
sometimes
walking with a
limp, so that we
always depend
on Him for
our needs.

THE HOLY SPIRIT IS A KIND MESSENGER. HE IS GIVING us all the opportunity to make wise decisions, to choose forgiveness, and to leave behind our sinful ways at this time. I urge you to let Jesus "dig in the garden of your heart now," and to let Him lead you in the process of sanctification and transformation. None of us are perfect, so that means there is always more. What areas of the garden of your heart is God working on in this season? Let soaking prayer be a time of heart healing.

_____

_____

_____

_____

_____

> People had incredible encounters with the Father, Son, and Holy Spirit; hearts were healed, marriages were restored, and people received vision and direction.

_____

_____

_____

_____

_____

_____

_____

_____

Many of us grow up believing that God is distant, critical, and angry, but as we get to know Him, our ideas about who He is and how He loves us change. We learn that He is kind, gentle, loving, and good. Do you believe Daddy God loves and accepts you? Do you believe He is a Good Father to you personally? If you're not sure or can't answer "yes" right away, this is an area to focus on in your soaking prayer times. Ask Daddy God to show you His goodness today.

_____

_____

_____

_____

_____

_____

> It spoke so deeply to my heart that the Father would stop what He's doing and would want to dance with His daughter. It drew my heart to Him.

_____

_____

_____

_____

_____

_____

_____

_____

_____

_____

_____

HAVE YOU EVER LOOKED IN THE MIRROR AND SAID, "I am so loved by Jesus. I am worthy. My Daddy God loves me." The first time you do it, it might be hard to look yourself in the eyes and believe it. The truth stops at your head and doesn't make its way to your heart. But as you soak, the truth of His love will sink in deep to your inner being. Ask God to give you one truth that He feels about you that you can speak over yourself today. Say it out loud in the mirror. Write it down on a sticky note so you see it every day. As you soak, listen to Him repeat the truth over you.

_____

_____

_____

_____

_____

_____

_____

_____

_____

_____

_____

_____

_____

_____

_____

_____

> I started to soak and to encounter the Holy Spirit, and I discovered His nearness and His love and His absolute delight in me and that built my confidence, bit by bit.

GOD WANTS TO BRING YOU PEACE WHERE THERE IS anxiety, and to bring you comfort where there is pain. He exchanges your concerns and worries for His love and peace. What is bringing you anxiety or pain today? Are you willing to offer this to God and let Him speak peace into your situation? He always has a good plan for your life. Nothing is impossible for our God!

> "Cast all your anxiety on him because he cares for you" (1 Peter 5:7 NIV).

IF WE WANT TO SEE MIRACLES, SIGNS, AND WONDERS, we must listen to what God wants to do, just as Jesus said and did what He heard and saw the Father saying and doing. Miracles don't always happen in the way that we expect. We have seen God use soaking prayer as a tool for healing many times. Often people receive a partial healing, and then when we soak them in prayer, even for many hours, they receive more and more healing. Do you need a physical healing? Are you willing to soak in His presence and ask Him to heal you?

_____

_____

_____

_____

_____

_____

_____

_____

_____

_____

_____

_____

_____

_____

_____

> With miracles, you're always walking on the water. It's about trust—putting your hand in His hand, knowing that Jesus paid the price for people to be healed.

When you're struggling through a difficult time, it's easy to become very inward focused. You spend so much time and energy dealing with the problems that you lose sight of God's goodness. If you're sick, if you're discouraged, or if you're in a wilderness season, can you make the decision to praise the Lord today? Bless Him, no matter what you feel like. As you turn your focus to Him, you'll feel His attention on you too.

James 3:10 says that you can't curse and bless God at the same time. I have learned how true that is. You can't be negative or irritated and praise God at the same time.

ACTIVATION AND PRAYER

Have you been disappointed when you have prayed and believed for your-self or someone else to be healed (physically or emotionally) and not seen any breakthrough? God knows your heart and wants to restore your hope today. If that's you, pray this from your heart:

God, it has been difficult seeing the people I love suffer from sickness and emotional pain and not be healed in the timing that I hoped for. It has been painful that You haven't brought my breakthrough yet. I've been disappointed and lost hope. I'm sorry for any lies that I have believed. God, would You renew my hope and faith for healing again? I want to see from Your perspective. I believe that it's always Your will to heal, so would You give me childlike faith to believe for healing again.

Do you need healing? As you soak, ask the Lord to heal your body:

Lord, You say that if we ask, You will answer. So, Lord, I ask today that You would come, that You would fill me and that You would allow me to love You and let You love me. I'm going to position myself today for healing. I ask You, Lord, to heal me, as I rest in Your presence.

SECTION 5

SOAKING UNTIL
WE SHINE

I REALLY BELIEVE THAT SOAKING IS A MAJOR KEY TO becoming more like Jesus. The more time you spend with Him, the more you'll get to know who He is, what He loves, and what He wants. That is how we will bring His Kingdom to earth and transform this world for His glory. In Exodus 34, we see that Moses spent time in the presence of God and his face shone:

> *So he was there with the Lord forty days and forty nights; he neither ate bread nor drank water. And He wrote on the tablets the words of the covenant, the Ten Commandments. Now it was so, when Moses came down from Mount Sinai (and the two tablets of the Testimony were in Moses' hand when he came down from the mountain), that Moses did not know that the skin of his face shone while he talked with Him. So when Aaron and all the children of Israel saw Moses, behold, the skin of his face shone, and they were afraid to come near him* (Exodus 34:28-30).

Moses was immersed so deeply in God's presence that his spirit, soul, and body was infused with the glory of God. He was radiating God's glory. Jesus is coming back for a bride who is compatible and comparable to Him. For the bride to be pleasing to the glorious Bridegroom, she must be glorious too. As a church, we become more glorious as we are immersed in God's presence, saturated and overflowing with love for Him and love for one another. Are you willing to surrender everything to become more like your Bridegroom King and shine His light into every dark place?

If you're not filled with God's presence, your efforts to love and serve other people will become striving, controlling, and manipulative.

DO YOU REMEMBER THE STORY OF MARY AND Martha? (See Luke 10.) Martha is working hard to prepare a feast for Jesus while her sister sits at His feet. She says, "Do you not care that my sister has left me to do all the work?" Jesus replies, "Martha, you are so troubled and so worried about many things. But one thing is needed and that will not be taken away from her. Mary has chosen the best." Mary valued time with Jesus, whereas Martha was serving and working, and Jesus rebuked her. It is not working hard for Jesus that transforms us to be like Him, it is sitting at His feet. Today, just soak at His feet and ask Him to take away all your striving.

> Intimacy with the Lord is about connecting with Him all the time.

PETER DENIED JESUS THREE TIMES, AND I'M SURE HE
thought, "I've blown it so badly that I'm never going to make
it. I'm going back to fishing." After Jesus was resurrected,
He stood with Peter, eating the fish, and commissioned
him three times. He restored Peter's hope and showed him
trust and love. Are there any places where you feel you've
messed up? Have you let that cause distance between you
and Jesus? Have you disqualified yourself to shine for Him?
Ask Him to show you how He sees you today.

Jesus, I position myself to hear what You want to say to me.

LET'S GO EVEN DEEPER INTO THE STORY OF PETER. Read John 21. Put yourself in Peter's shoes and imagine how much shame he must have felt after denying Jesus right before His death. Now imagine how much love he must have felt as Jesus rebuilt trust with him. That is the love and compassion that the Father wants to show you when you mess up. A lot of us will let the Lord love us when we feel like we deserve it, if we've really been praying, reading the Bible, and serving Him. If we've been too busy for those things, we feel like we haven't earned His love. We forget that Jesus paid the ultimate price for us to have a relationship with the Father. Ask God to reveal that forgiveness, love, and acceptance to your heart today.

> I realized that it was Jesus talking to me. I suddenly knew that He loved me in all my sin, in all my fears, and in all my pain.

Every time Jesus related to the disciples, it was a clear representation of how the Father wants to relate to them, and to us, too. Jesus taught the disciples that prayer is agreeing with what the Father wants, that it is a relational thing. The Father wants us to pray in the same way that Jesus showed the disciples, where we can come boldly before Him, like little children, asking Him what He wants and declaring it back to Him. As you soak, ask Him to show you the prayers on His heart.

_____

_____

_____

_____

_____

> Jesus said that He only did what He saw the Father doing and He only said what He heard the Father saying (see John 5:19). I want to continually remember to pray that prayer.

_____

_____

_____

_____

_____

_____

_____

_____

_____

_____

_____

_____

SMITH WIGGLESWORTH SAID, "IF YOU ARE IN HIS love, you will be swallowed up with holy desire. You will have no desire, only the Lord. Your mind will be filled with divine reflection. Your whole heart will be taken up with things that pertain to the Kingdom of God, and you will live in the secret place of the Most High, and you will abide there." Meditate on this quote today as you soak.

> We can do all sorts of good things, but without love, it's worth nothing.

I BELIEVE THAT THE NEXT WAVE OF HIM MOVING IS going to be a holiness wave. God is looking for people who will be so consumed by Him that they literally become the shining ones. God chose you to represent Him on the earth. Leave behind all that hinders you and step into this wave of His holiness and glory.

> God is love and
> He wants us
> to be lovers.

ACTIVATION AND PRAYER

When John and I began soaking prayer, God told us to give Him our mornings. In an act of faith, we cancelled all our morning appointments just to be with Him. Every morning we'd spend our time in prayer, in the Word, and in His presence. It was such a joy to intentionally carve out that time for the Lord. Some mornings were filled with intimacy, some were full of new revelation. On other mornings, nothing seemed to happen at all, but we kept going because obedience to God's call was so important to us. These times changed our lives and our ministry.

The most valuable thing we have to give is our time. Matthew 6:21 says, *"Where your treasure is, there your heart will be also."* The way you use your time will always show what's most important to you.

What if God is asking you to make a radical change in how you spend your time? Throughout this journal you've made time to be with God, but what if He is asking for even more? What if it is hours a day? Beloved, are you willing to be so obedient and so in tune with His heart? Pray this with me:

> *God I am willing. Whatever it looks like. I want to be one of Your shining ones like Moses and Mary and Peter. Help me to leave behind all that hinders me and sit at Your feet in worship, then take Your love to the lost ones. Let me shine for You, Jesus.*

I believe the Body of Christ is stepping into a new wave of God's holiness. It means we will have to leave behind old ways of thinking and step into the new. That is what happened in Toronto when revival came. It was beyond anything we could have asked or imagined. We had to walk hand in hand with the Lord because we didn't know what would happen from one meeting to the next.

God has so much more for you than all you could ask or imagine. I pray that as you have taken this soaking journey you have gone to deep places with Him. As we close this journal, I will leave you with a powerful revelation God spoke to me as the revival began. Allow this to be an invitation for even more of all He has for you.

> *Tell my people that this is a time when I'm pouring out the oil of My Spirit and they are to be like the five wise virgins in Matthew 25. They all were looking for the soon coming of the Lord. They all carried lamps. They all had them lit. They all slumbered and slept. But what was the difference between the five wise and the five foolish? The five wise had extra oil. This is a time when I am pouring out the oil of My Spirit. It's going to cost them to buy oil—and have extra oil and the cost is vulnerability, humility, and pressing into intimacy.*

ABOUT CAROL ARNOTT

Carol Arnott, and her husband John, are the founding pastors of Catch the Fire—formerly known as the Toronto Airport Christian Fellowship—and overseers of the Catch The Fire Partners network of churches. As international speakers, John and Carol have become known for their ministry of revival in the context of the Father's saving and restoring love. As the Holy Spirit moves with signs and wonders, they have seen millions of lives touched and changed through God's power and Christ's love.

Manufactured by Amazon.ca
Bolton, ON